A PLACE IN HISTORY

the White HOUSE

Author: Karen Price Hossell
Consultant: Adam Smith

ticktock
MEDIA

Copyright © *ticktock* Entertainment Ltd 2005
First published in Great Britain in 2005 by *ticktock* Media Ltd.,
Unit 2, Orchard Business Centre, North Farm Road, Tunbridge Wells, Kent, TN2 3XF
We would like to thank: Alison Howard, Susan Barraclough, Jenni Rainford and Elizabeth Wiggans for their help with
this book.
ISBN 1 86007 599 1 PB
Printed in China
A CIP catalogue record for this book is available from the British Library.

Contents

Introduction

Although it is only just over 200 years old – young compared with other historical buildings around the world – the White House is rich in history. More than 40 presidents and their families have lived there since November, 1800, when President John Adams and his wife became its first residents.

A NEW CAPITAL

Before the White House was built, the official home of the United States president was first in New York City, then in Philadelphia. But early on in American history, government leaders decided they wanted their headquarters to be more centrally located, so they purchased a strip of land where the borders of Virginia and Maryland met and began planning the new capital city. They decided to call the region the District of Columbia, and later agreed to call the city Washington, after President George Washington. One of the first buildings that should be erected, they agreed, was the president's home.

The government held a contest, inviting architects to submit plans for the new president's home. The winner was an Irish

This painting of George Washington was saved from a White House fire by First Lady Dolley Madison in 1814 (see p. 11).

architect named James Hoban. The cornerstone was laid in 1792, and construction was completed in 1800. Along with Hoban, President Washington oversaw much of the mansion's construction. However, he died in 1799, less than a year before it was finished.

MANY LIVES

Over its 200-year history, hundreds of lives have been led inside the White House. Its rooms have resonated with the sounds of laughter and song, of barking dogs and dancing feet. Children have slid down the banisters of the Grand Staircase and romped on the Great Lawn. Dignitaries from all over the world have attended dinners and concerts in the State Dining Room, as well as serious meetings in the Cabinet Room. Brides and grooms have become wives and husbands in wedding ceremonies inside the White House and on its grounds. Sometimes, the silence of sorrow has filled the White House as well, when family members and presidents themselves have died.

As the United States grew from a small, fledgling nation into the most powerful force in the modern world, the White House grew as well. Today, the White House is probably the most recognisable building in the United States. To most Americans, it symbolises the strength and dignity of the presidency.

The White House has been home to many children of all ages, such as John F. Kennedy Jr., pictured here with his father.

CHAPTER 1

How it was built

I n the late 18th century, the artist and engineer Pierre Charles L'Enfant worked with George Washington on the plans for a new American capital city. L'Enfant thought the president's home should be built on a grand scale like a European palace. The Irish architect James Hoban won a competition to design the building, and a workforce – consisting mainly of slaves – took eight years to build it.

The winning design for the new president's home was drawn by Irish architect, James Hoban.

A HOUSE FIT FOR A LEADER

In 1790 the lawmaking body of the United States, called Congress, passed the Residency Act. The Act provided for the establishment of a new city, to be called Washington. The city would be on a nine-mile square square piece of land on the shores of the Potomac River between the states of Virginia and Maryland. The precise location was personally selected by President Washington. The region the city was in was to be called the District of Columbia. Artist and engineer Pierre Charles L'Enfant worked with George Washington on the plans for the city. L'Enfant was born in France and was a Major in the United States Army during the American Revolution.

One of the first buildings to be constructed in Washington would be the home for the president. Congress determined that by 1800 the home should be ready to house the president and his family. In his design of the city, L'Enfant set aside 33 hectares for what he called the 'President's Park'. After the site was selected, leaders began to plan the buildings.

THE WINNING ARCHITECT

The Secretary of State, Thomas Jefferson, announced a competition to design the new president's home. Nine architects submitted plans for the president's mansion, and James Hoban won the competition. Hoban was born

This early drawing of the White House shows the crowd gathered for Andrew Jackson's inauguration in 1829.

Tales & customs – ANGLO-PALLADIAN STYLE

The Anglo-Palladian architectural style is known for its square, geometric form. The front centre of a building designed in this style usually has a kind of porch called a 'portico' with four columns and curved stairs on either side. The buildings are symmetrical, with matching windows on either side. Inside the front door of the building would be a large entrance hall with a grand staircase.

in Ireland, and his design was based on a building in the city of Dublin, Ireland, called Leinster House. The grand house was built in what is called the 'Anglo-Palladian' style, based on the works of the 16th-century Italian architect Andrea Palladio. English architects used many of his ideas in their designs. The president's

mansion was also influenced by Georgian architecture, named after King George III, who was on the throne when the style became popular.

Once his plan was selected, Hoban moved to Washington, DC, and began to oversee the construction of the president's

President George Washington oversaw the bulk of the building of the White House.

mansion. He worked closely with President George Washington on the design. Hoban thought the president's house should have two stories and a raised basement. The building would be constructed from sandstone. The cornerstone of the building was laid on October 13, 1792. Stonemasons were brought in from Scotland to carve the large blocks of sandstone used to construct the outside shell of the building. Few builders in America were used to working with sandstone, but Scottish

The White House

This 18th-century engraving of stonemasons at work gives us an idea of the tools and methods that would have been used when building the White House. Stonemasons were recruited from Scotland and the majority of the labour was carried out by slaves.

stonemasons had perfected techniques of carving and laying the stone over hundreds of years.

SOLID AS A ROCK

President Washington had very specific ideas about how he wanted the president's house to look. In the 18th century, most homes were built from wood. Some American leaders of the day thought the president's new home should be built from brick, but because it represented the strength and stability of the new nation, Washington thought the president's house should be built out of solid stone.

The ornamental carvings around the windows and on other parts of the façade, Washington determined, should also be made of stone. The idea of stone carvings of rosettes and other decorations deviated from the usual Anglo-Palladian style, but Washington wanted to

Tales & customs — ALL IN THE NAME

Until 1902, 'White House' was not the official name of the president's home. Until then it was sometimes called the White House, but it was more often called the 'Executive Mansion'. The exterior walls were made from a greyish-brown sandstone, but when whitewashed in 1798, the name 'White House' began to be more commonly used. In 1901, President Theodore Roosevelt had the words 'White House' printed on his presidential stationery, making the name official.

incorporate some of his own preferences into the design.

THE LABOURERS

Besides stonemasons recruited from Scotland, other labourers were hired to work on the home, as well, including slaves. Slavery

The plaster façade is intricately designed down to every detail.

had been in existence in the American colonies since about the middle of the 17th century, and Virginia and Maryland, the two states that had given up parcels of land to make up the District of Columbia, employed a great deal of slave labour.

At first the commissioners of the District of Columbia planned to hire labourers from the United States and Europe, but few workers responded to their advertisements, so they soon decided to use slaves. African-American slaves not only built most of the White House, but other government buildings in Washington, DC, as well, including the Capitol.

From the beginning of construction in 1792 until November of 1800, the labourers worked every year during the milder months, from early spring to late autumn. The workers lived in shacks on the grounds, and the ground round the president's new home was muddy and littered with trash from the workers and with left-over construction supplies. The building itself was constructed

using a technique that had been in place for thousands of years. The outer layer of stone that can be seen when you look at the White House is backed by a layer of brick. This type of construction ensures that the White House is solidly built, which is one reason the building still stands after more than two hundred years.

AQUIA SANDSTONE

The type of sandstone used to build the White House is called Aquia sandstone, which is a combination of quartz sand, pebbles and clay pellets, held together by a sandy substance called silica. The sandstone came from a quarry along the Potomac River in Virginia. In 1791, L'Enfant was charged by Congress to find a source for the sandstone, and he purchased for the US government the Wiggington's Island quarry alongside the Aquia Creek in Virginia.

The special stone used for the White House is called Aquia sandstone, the same material used for this column – one of the 'Capitol Columns' monument that stands at the National Arboretum in Washington, DC.

Known for many years as simply the 'Executive Mansion', the White House has been a symbol of America's presidency and government for more than 200 years. While bearing witness to much political history, the White House has also endured two serious fires and various terrorist threats. All the while, the historic landmark has absorbed something of the personalities of its inhabitants, through its many makeovers and renovations.

John Adams was the first US president to live at the White House. When he first moved in, the mansion was far from finished.

FIRST RESIDENTS

George Washington died in 1799 and so never had a chance to see the completed building he helped to design. His successor, President John Adams and his wife, Abigail, were the first residents at the White House. John Adams was one of the main leaders in America's fight for independence, and his greatest presidential achievement was avoiding war with France through lengthy negotiations. This cool-headed, dignified way of diverting the war threat came in the midst of public feeling that war was necessary. However, Adams maintained that there was nothing to be gained through going to war.

The Adamses moved into the White House during November of 1800, even though it was not quite finished. When they first saw the building, they may have been disappointed. There were almost no buildings in Washington, DC at the time and no landscaping or gardens around the mansion. The shacks used by the work crews still stood on the muddy, littered grounds. The plaster used to coat the walls of the house was still wet, and 36 of the rooms had not been plastered at all. The exterior walls of the building were a greyish-white – the house was not painted white for several years.

ADVOCATE FOR FREEDOM

In 1801, former secretary of state Thomas Jefferson became president. Jefferson was a brilliant and inventive man who was a firm believer in the human right to freedom. Although highly

Time line

1776	America issues the Declaration of Independence.	
1783	Treaty of Paris is signed. Britain recognises American independence following the American Revolution.	
1787	The new Constitution is drafted and ratified by the individual states the following year.	
1789	George Washington becomes first president of USA.	

1790	A new capital city location is chosen and named Washington.	
1792	Thomas Jefferson announces competition to design new president's house. Irish architect, James Hoban wins.	
1800	President John Adams moves into the new residence which is known as the President's House or Executive Mansion.	
1801	The President's House is opened to the public on January 1.	

The Declaration of Independence was drafted by Benjamin Franklin, John Adams and Thomas Jefferson.

intelligent, Jefferson was not comfortable with public speaking and often did his work behind the scenes, such as when he drafted the Declaration of Independence, one of his greatest achievements.

A lover of architecture, when a contest for designs for the new President's House was announced, Jefferson anonymously submitted a design of his own. Jefferson made several additions to the President's House including redesigning the garden, planting hundreds of trees. He built a wall around the house and oversaw the construction of colonnades that led from the eastern and western sides of the house.

LUCKY SAVE

The next residents were James Madison and his wife, Dolley. Dolley was popular with the public and a great hostess at White House parties. After ongoing disputes over trade President Madison declared war on Britain in 1812. America, only recently independent, was unprepared for war. On August 24, 1814, Dolley and members of her staff were alerted that British troops were invading Washington, DC. The Madisons prepared to flee but before they left, Dolley insisted on saving a portrait of George Washington. Today, the painting hangs in the East Room of the White House.

That night, British troops set the President's House on fire. The flames destroyed the inside of the house, although most of the exterior walls remained standing. James Hoban, the architect who had designed the President's House, stepped in once more to oversee the reconstruction. After the house was burned, many Americans were outraged, and they united in a renewed sense of patriotism.

First Lady Madison saved a number of important documents and a painting of George Washington before the White House was set on fire by British troops in 1814.

	Thomas Jefferson becomes the new president.
1803	Louisiana Purchase Treaty is signed.
1809	James Madison becomes president.
1812	America declares war on Britain and France.
1814	Britain invades Washington and set fire to the White House. The Madisons salvage some things, including a portrait of George Washington.

President Abraham Lincoln was most famous for issuing the 'Emancipation Proclamation' in 1861, which called for an end to slavery across America.

AN END TO SLAVERY

Republican president Abraham Lincoln was the 15th president to live at the White House. Six weeks after becoming president, Civil War began. The northern states of America (or the Union) fought against the southern states (known as the Confederacy). At issue was slavery – the northern states believed that slaves should be freed while the southern states disagreed. Perhaps even more important to those in the Union was the idea that the union of states that they tried so hard to build was threatened, thus weakening the strength of the nation. In 1861, as the outbreak of war became imminent, Lincoln turned the East Room of the White House into temporary barracks for soldiers about to join the cause.

Lincoln believed there should be an end to slavery and in 1863, his Emancipation Proclamation was

When Theodore Roosevelt invited the African-American educator Booker T. Washington to dine at the White House, the public were outraged.

Time line				
	1823	Monroe Doctrine is signed, which instructs European countries not to intervene in the West.	1865	President Lincoln is assassinated.
	1861	Abraham Lincoln becomes president. With Civil War about to erupt, soldiers are temporarily housed in the White House's East Room.	1874	King David Kalakaua of the Sandwich Islands (Hawaii) is the first ruling monarch to visit the White House.
			1877	First telephone is installed for President Rutherford B. Hayes.
	1863	President Lincoln signs the Emancipation Proclamation.	1901	The President's House is officially renamed the

published, which declared that all slaves should be freed in the southern states. The war lasted from 1861 until 1865, when the Union gained victory and slavery was finally abolished. In 1865, Lincoln was assassinated by John Wilkes Booth, who believed he was helping the Confederate cause. Lincoln's body was placed in a casket in the East Room before his funeral.

NO STRANGER TO CONTROVERSY

When President Theodore Roosevelt and his large family moved into the White House in 1901, the building was bursting at the seams. He moved his family to a home on Lafayette Square in Washington while architects, engineers and construction workers built a new wing on the west side of the White House. The wing would house the office of future presidents, cabinet and staff, as well as the press room – making more room elsewhere for the presidential family to live. The youngest president to date, Roosevelt was a modern-minded president who introduced a

President Woodrow Wilson and First Lady Edith Bolling Wilson are pictured here on Armistice Day, 1918.

more assertive foreign policy and other progressive reforms. He was also sometimes controversial, such as when he invited African American educator Booker T. Washington to a White House dinner. Roosevelt thought Washington was an impressive man who would be an interesting guest. Even 40 years after the end of slavery, most white Americans at the time held deeply racist views and were offended by this public recognition of a black man.

THE BURDEN OF WAR

Woodrow Wilson became president in 1913. Like Roosevelt before him, Wilson was another passionate believer in democracy. He was re-elected for a second term, partly because of his campaign slogan; 'He kept us out of war' – as World War I had been fought for three years without any involvement from the USA. However, in 1917, Wilson concluded that he could no longer, in good conscience, hold that stance. After three American ships were sunk by German U-boats in the North Atlantic, Wilson requested permission from Congress to declare war on Germany. The support America lent to the Allies helped to bring Germany to eventual defeat in 1918.

	'White House' by President Theodore Roosevelt.
1902	The White House undergoes its first major renovation and expansion to make way for the large Roosevelt family. West Wing is built.
1909	The Oval Office and Cabinet Room are added to the West Wing.
1913	The first press conference to take place at the White House is given by President Woodrow Wilson.

The White House

President Wilson gave the first ever press conference from the White House in 1913. Wilson declared that from then on the president would give; '... full and free discussion of all large questions of the moment.'

LOYALTY AND OPTIMISM

When Franklin D. Roosevelt became president in 1933, it was the middle of The Great Depression, when 13 million people were unemployed.

President Franklin D. Roosevelt met British Prime Minister Winston Churchill for a secret meeting aboard a battleship, which resulted in the Anglo-American alliance during World War II.

Roosevelt helped to boost morale by introducing a national recovery programme.

On December 24, 1929, during Herbert Hoover's presidency, fire destroyed the West Wing of the White House. Roosevelt took this opportunity to have the Oval Office moved from the centre of the building to the southeast corner. This was so that the office could have windows, and so the president could get to the West Wing in privacy. Interestingly, the White House was one of the first public buildings in America to be equipped with disabled access-ways due to president Roosevelt suffering from polio.

When war broke out once more in Europe, Roosevelt offered complete assistance to Britain and the Allies, but stopped short of sending troops to the front. However, when Japan attacked Pearl Harbor in 1941, Roosevelt declared war on Japan and Germany. In 1942, during Roosevelt's administration, an East Wing was added to the White House. Today, the wing

President Truman had to make some of the most difficult decisions in US political history, such as the decision to bomb Japan towards the end of World War II.

houses the offices of the First Lady and the Emergency Operations Center which is located in a bunker beneath the East Wing.

TRUMAN PERIOD

Following the death of Franklin D. Roosevelt while in office, the next president was Harry S. Truman, who was thrust into one

Time line		
1914–1918 World War I takes place.	**1942**	East Wing added to White House.
1929 Fire destroys the West Wing of the White House.	**1945**	President Roosevelt dies while in office. Japan surrenders after Truman drops bombs on the Japanese cities of Hiroshima and Nagasaki, ending World War II. Truman orders the signing of the United Nations Charter.
1933 President Franklin D. Roosevelt gives first 'fireside chat' radio broadcast.		
1939 World War II begins.		
1941 Japan attacks Pearl Harbor.	**1949**	Three-year structural renovation of the White House begins.

of the most trying times in US presidential history when he took up office in 1945. Shortly after becoming president, Truman made the decision to try to end the war by dropping atomic bombs on the Japanese cities of Hiroshima and Nagasaki. Japan soon surrendered after the devastation these weapons caused. In June, 1945, Harry Truman ordered the signing of the Charter of the United Nations. He also set up a military organisation called NATO (North Atlantic Treaty Organization) to protect western nations from the perceived communist threat. In 1950, Truman committed troops to another war, aiding South Korea in fighting against the communist North Korea.

Like his leadership decisions, President Truman's ideas for improving the White House were also met with controversy. By the middle of the 20th century, the White House was so structurally weak that one of the legs of a piano owned by President Truman's daughter Margaret fell through her bedroom floor to the ceiling of the family dining room below. Despite historians'

John F. Kennedy and his wife Jacqueline made an enormous impact during their period in the White House. They were undoubtedly the most glamorous couple the White House had seen and Jacqueline made radical changes to the mansion's décor.

apprehensions, between 1949 and 1952, the White House underwent its most major renovation ever. At Truman's request, a balcony was built on the south front of the White House. This decision was controversial because many thought it ruined Hoban's original design.

PROMISING CAREER CUT SHORT

The young and dashing John F. Kennedy took up office in 1961, and the White House changed greatly during his presidency. His wife, Jacqueline, was considered to be among the most elegant of all of the first ladies. Even before she moved into the White House, Mrs. Kennedy began to research ideas about how to redecorate it. At the time, many of the White House furnishings were reproductions of American antiques, and she was determined to replace them with original American antiques. People from all over the United States donated furniture to her cause. By 1962, the White House had been completely revamped. With popular American broadcaster Walter Cronkite, Mrs. Kennedy unveiled the newly furnished White House in a television programme broadcast to the American public.

Richard Nixon hugs his daughter Julie upon making the decision that he will resign as President of the United States.

President Kennedy faced a potential crisis in October 1962, when American spy planes discovered that Soviet nuclear missiles were set up in Cuba and aimed at the United States. After much negotiation, Kennedy and his advisors were able to settle the crisis with the Soviet Union, who removed the missiles.

Kennedy's potential as a great leader was cut short when on November 22, 1963, he was assassinated by Lee Harvey Oswald in Dallas, Texas. Kennedy's body was taken back to Washington DC, and his casket was placed in the White House until his funeral.

AN UNSETTLING TIME

Six years after Kennedy's death, Richard Nixon became president. Nixon's years were marred by the ongoing and unpopular Vietnam War and the Watergate scandal. This involved officials in President Nixon's Republican re-election committee, who broke into Democratic headquarters at the Watergate Hotel in Washington, DC, to steal documents to help them spy on their opponent's campaign strategies. After a lengthy trial, several Republican leaders were convicted, and others resigned. Although Nixon ended the Vietnam War in 1973, the Watergate scandal caused him to resign in 1974, becoming the first president in American history to do so.

The former movie star Ronald Reagan became president in 1981 and held the post until 1989. Perhaps the most notable achievement of President Reagan's presidency was improving relations between the two superpowers. Reagan's moves towards peace with the Soviet leader Mikhail Gorbachev also allowed him to concentrate on

Charismatic president, Bill Clinton's term in office was marred by a personal scandal.

Time line		
1968	Black Civil Rights activist Martin Luther King Jr and US Senator Robert Kennedy are assassinated.	
1973	US troops withdrawn from Vietnam.	
1974	Richard Nixon is the first president to resign from office.	
1981	President Reagan survives an assassination attempt.	
1990	The Gulf War begins.	
1991	A US-led coalition launches an air-strike on Iraq. Persian Gulf War takes place. Iraq is defeated.	
1992	US President George HW Bush and Russian President Boris Yeltsin issue a joint statement declaring that their countries no longer 'regard each other as potential adversaries.'	

cutting taxes at home in the US. Reagan's vice president, George HW Bush, became president in 1989. Perhaps the most notable event of his presidency was the Persian Gulf War, which took place after Iraq invaded Kuwait in the Middle East. When Iraqi troops seemed poised to invade the oil-rich Middle East, the United Nations ordered Saddam to pull back his troops. He ignored the warnings, and in 1991 coalition troops attacked Iraq. When the war ended a few weeks later, many believed that trouble would not be over until Saddam Hussein was removed from power.

During the presidency of Bill Clinton, which lasted from 1993 to 2001, the United States enjoyed a strong economy and a time of peace. However, because of his involvement in a personal scandal, Clinton was impeached by the House of Representatives, meaning that they accused him of having committed, in the words of the Constitution, '... high crimes and misdemeanors' that brought his presidency into disrepute. The other lawmaking body of the

President George W. Bush decided to commit US troops to war with Iraq after Saddam Hussein repeatedly failed to co-operate with experts looking for weapons of mass destruction.

United States, the Senate, found Clinton not guilty, and so he continued as president. In 1998, Clinton ordered the bombing of Iraq when its leader, Saddam Hussein, would not co-operate with UN inspectors, who were charged with examining warehouses in Iraq for evidence of illegal weapons.

TERRORIST THREAT

Eight years after President Bush left office, one of his sons, George W. Bush, became president. During his first year as president, the United States was a victim of a violent act of terrorism when, on September 11, 2001, terrorists

from a group called al-Qaeda hijacked jetliners and flew them into the World Trade Center in New York City and the Pentagon in Washington, DC. The White House was likely to have been the target of a plane that crashed into a field in Pennsylvania after passengers tried to overcome the hijackers. President Bush took action against al-Qaeda, sending troops to its bases in Afghanistan. Not long after that war was over, the US – along with many allies including Britain, Italy, Poland, France and Germany – agreed it was necessary to invade Iraq. Saddam Hussein was eventually captured in late 2003. The invasion of Iraq was controversial in the United States as well as around the world. The George W. Bush administration claimed it knew for certain that Saddam had weapons of mass destruction. To date, however, no evidence has actually been recovered.

1993	World Trade Center is bombed but only minimal damage is caused.
1998	Bill Clinton is charged with lying in court and faces impeachment.
2001	An Islamic militant group called Al Qaeda bombs the World Trade Center in New York and the Pentagon in Washington. President Bush sends troops into Afghanistan, and shortly afterwards into Iraq.
2003	Saddam Hussein is captured by US troops and imprisoned in Iraq.

CHAPTER 3   *Explore the White House*

The White House, situated between Pennsylvania Avenue and Constitution Avenue in Washington DC, is so much more than the centre of American power and government. It is a living treasure trove of history, art, furnishings and memories. Echoes of past presidents and their families remain – visible in the portrait galleries and personal touches that linger from the various terms of office through the decades. The mansion still provides a home to the current president and his family. And what a magnificent home it is.

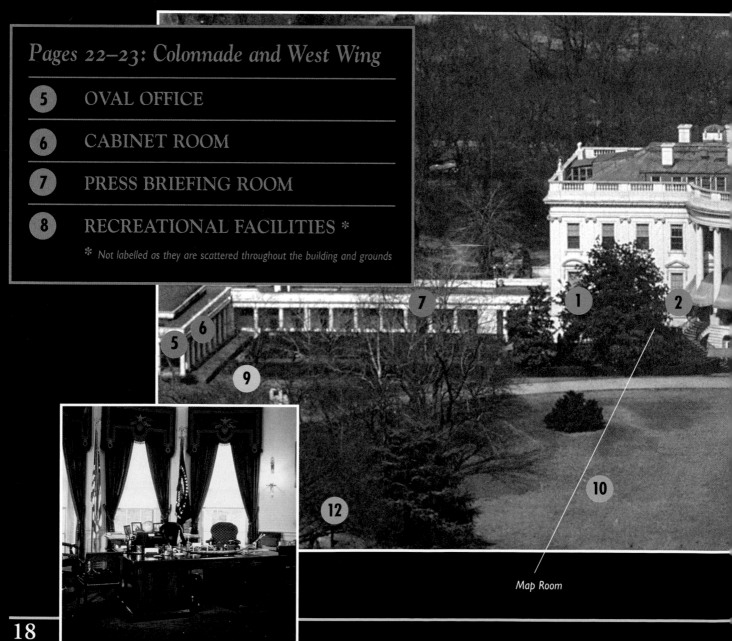

Map Room

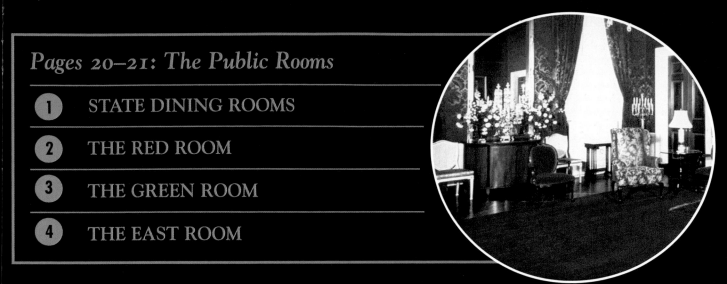

Pages 20–21: *The Public Rooms*

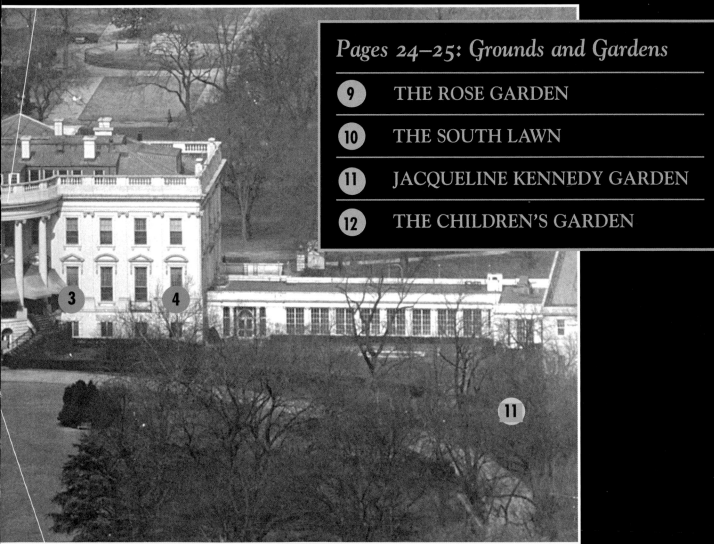

South Portico

Pages 24–25: *Grounds and Gardens*

Blue Room

The room at the southwest corner of the Public Rooms is the State Dining Room. Notable pieces of silverware and glassware grace the large mahogany table. This is how the room looked in 1961.

① STATE DINING ROOM

The **STATE DINING ROOM** can seat as many as 140 guests. The magnificent gilded bronze centrepiece bought by President Monroe often graces the table. The room was enlarged when President Theodore Roosevelt had the West Wing built in 1902. To accommodate more guests, the long mahogany table is often replaced by smaller tables.

The Red Room has assumed many different purposes and styles over the years. The picture above shows the room as it looked in the 1950s.

② THE RED ROOM

The **RED ROOM** is furnished in the Empire Style of the early 19th century and is currently used as a reception room. First Lady Jackie Kennedy styled the room, and her decor has been maintained over the years. In 1902 the walls were covered with red satin fabric with a gold design on the border. Today, the carpet is beige, red and gold. In the early 1900s, the room was a playroom for Theodore Roosevelt's children. From 1933, First Lady Eleanor Roosevelt held press conferences for women reporters in the Red Room.

③ THE GREEN ROOM

Thomas Jefferson used the **GREEN ROOM** as a dining room, but today it is a small parlour that is a good place for quiet conversation. It has been the site of small gatherings and even televised interviews. The walls are covered in green silk, and the furniture is from the earliest years of the White House, although none of it is original to the mansion. Among the paintings in the room is a New Jersey beach scene by Henry Tanner, the first African-American to have work displayed in the White House.

The Green Room as it was decorated in 1952 during President Eisenhower's administration.

④ THE EAST ROOM

The **EAST ROOM** is the largest room in the White House and has served many functions, including being used as a movie theatre. When he designed the White House, James Hoban intended the East Room as a public-audience room. The room contains three chandeliers, each of which has more than 6,000 pieces of glass. The painting of George Washington by Gilbert Stuart, saved by Dolley Madison in 1814, hangs in the East Room. It is the only item in the White House that has remained there since 1800.

The East Room's Steinway piano and large open floor make it a good choice of room for music recitals. This is how the room looked in 1948.

The famous Oval Office has its shape so that many of the president's advisors can gather around his desk at one time.

5 OVAL OFFICE

The president's office, otherwise known as the **OVAL OFFICE**, is the best-known room in the West Wing. Each president or first lady designs a rug for the office, with the presidential seal. The president can select which paintings he wants to hang on the walls. George W. Bush, for example, chose several paintings of his home state of Texas, along with portraits of Abraham Lincoln and George Washington. John F. Kennedy, on the other hand, decorated the walls with naval paintings and watercolours. Jacqueline Kennedy chose red carpet for the office and, ironically, it was being fitted at the very moment that her husband was assassinated.

6 CABINET ROOM

Many serious meetings take place in the **CABINET ROOM**, where members of the president's cabinet, the National Security Council, members of Congress, and heads of state meet to discuss national and world issues. The room holds an oval mahogany table and leather chairs, and each member of the Cabinet is assigned a seat according to when his or her department was established.

Each chair in the Cabinet Room has a small plaque indicating who sits where. The president and vice president's chairs are further distinguished by having slightly higher backs.

7 PRESS BRIEFING ROOM

The **PRESS BRIEFING ROOM** was built above the pool that Franklin Roosevelt used – in the colonnade that leads to the west wing. In 2000, 29 kilometres of cable were laid under the floor to accommodate technological requirements. Every day, members of the press come to the room to learn the latest news from the White House. At the front of the room is a podium in front of blue draperies and the seal of the White House. Usually, the White House Press Secretary conducts press briefings. The journalists who gather for the daily briefing are called the White House Press Corps.

President Clinton delivers a speech before the distinctive seal and curtain of the Press Briefing Room.

8 RECREATIONAL FACILITIES

As Franklin D. Roosevelt's pool had been turned into the Press Briefing Room, in 1975 President Ford had another swimming pool built. Other **RECREATIONAL FACILITIES** at the White House include a bowling alley lane, a tennis court, a jogging track, a movie theatre, a golf practise green and a billiards room.

Every President needs some time off. In this picture President Nixon is captured stepping over the foul line as he delivers his ball down one of the White House bowling lanes.

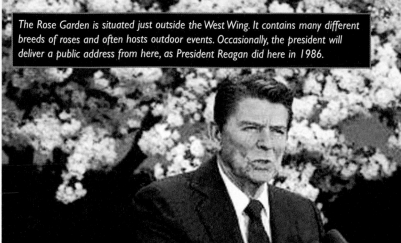

The Rose Garden is situated just outside the West Wing. It contains many different breeds of roses and often hosts outdoor events. Occasionally, the president will deliver a public address from here, as President Reagan did here in 1986.

9 THE ROSE GARDEN

The **ROSE GARDEN**, otherwise known as the West Garden, is perhaps the best-known area on White House grounds. The garden was begun by First Lady Ellen Wilson, Woodrow Wilson's first wife, in 1913. During the Kennedy Administration the garden was redesigned so it could be used for outdoor ceremonies. Besides roses, the garden has several types of tulips, grape hyacinth, lavender cotton and crabapple trees. Occasionally, the president will give speeches, hold ceremonies, or make announcements here.

10 THE SOUTH LAWN

The large expanse of grass on the south side of the White House is called the **SOUTH LAWN**. Sometimes, elaborate marquees are set up on the lawn for parties and concerts. The South Lawn is also the site of the annual Easter Egg Roll.

Many past Presidents and First Ladies have planted trees and shrubs on the South Lawn.

The East Garden was dedicated by Lady Bird Johnson to Jacqueline Kennedy in 1965.

11 THE JACQUELINE KENNEDY GARDEN

Like the Rose Garden, the **JACQUELINE KENNEDY GARDEN** is based on traditional 18th-century American garden design. The idea for the garden came from the Kennedys, and after President Kennedy's assassination, Lady Bird Johnson completed the plan and dedicated the garden to Mrs. Kennedy. The garden is framed by a holly hedge and planted with holly trees, tulips, pansies, and grape hyacinth. It also includes a herb garden that is used by White House chefs.

12 THE CHILDREN'S GARDEN

President and Mrs. Lyndon B. Johnson presented the **CHILDREN'S GARDEN** to the White House. It has a goldfish pond, an apple tree, and a paved area that has footprints and handprints of past presidents' children and grandchildren.

The Children's Garden was President and Mrs Johnson's idea for capturing memories of presidential children through the decades.

CHAPTER 4

The people

The White House has seen many people come and go since it was first occupied by President John Adams in 1800. More than 40 presidents and their families have called the big house home since then, arguably spending the most important years of their lives there. Besides the presidents, there have been the many first ladies and children. And, of course, the first families had to bring their pets with them to their new home.

AN INDEPENDENT MAN

Thomas Jefferson became president in 1801, at which time he was already connected to the President's House. Not only was he secretary of state under George Washington, but he participated in the contest held to select a design for the building and even submitted his own plan.

While Jefferson is known to have disliked the grandness of the White House, some think he added to it by hiring workers to install more carved garlands, wreaths, and other decorations above doors and around windows. Jefferson oversaw perhaps the greatest land purchase the United States ever made when, in 1803, Napoleon agreed to sell Louisiana – which comprised much of what is now the central western United States – to help fund his war in Europe. Soon after the purchase, Jefferson sent Meriwether Lewis and William Clark on an expedition to discover what lay west of the Mississippi. As they travelled, they sent back artifacts, including animal pelts, Native American objects, plant specimens, and animal bones. Jefferson displayed these in the entrance hall of the White House which was open to public view.

THE MADISONS

The next president was James Madison. He was a popular politician and played a large role in the development of the US Constitution. His wife Dolley was also well-liked and considered to be an excellent hostess.

The four presidents whose faces are carved into Mt Rushmore – George Washington, Thomas Jefferson, Theodore Roosevelt and Abraham Lincoln – represent the first 150 years of the US presidency.

President Andrew Johnson, who served from 1865 to 1869, sometimes hosted children's parties at the White House. One White House staffer, Colonel William H. Crook, wrote about one of them: 'There has never been a children's party so wonderful … The dancing was in the East Room. There were a great many square dances, and a few waltzes and polkas; but the fancy dances were the best …'.

Thomas Jefferson is best remembered for drafting the Declaration of Independence.

In fact, she was a popular guest at White House functions well after her husband's death. Because the State Dining Room was so cold, the Madisons had a furnace installed in the White House basement.

THE HUGE CHEESE

While Andrew Jackson, the seventh president, is known for his war heroism, perhaps one of the more infamous incidents that occurred during his presidency concerned a giant wheel of cheese. Weighing more than 635 kilograms, the cheddar was a gift from a Jackson supporter in New York. The cheese sat in the White House Entrance Hall for more than two years, and in the weeks before Jackson left office he invited the public to come and have a taste. It took only two hours for the cheese to be devoured. However, White House staff claimed that it took several years for the odour to go away and for the stain left by the cheese on the floor to be removed.

A statue of President Andrew Jackson stands near the White House in Washington, DC.

27

The White House

SOLDIERS IN THE EAST ROOM

Abraham Lincoln is one of the most well-known and loved of the American presidents. He endured much sadness during his four years in the White House. Besides the tragic death of his middle son, Willie, Lincoln had to watch the nation he loved split apart by political differences as the Civil War took place during most of his presidency. When Lincoln called for troops to sign up to fight for the Union in 1861, thousands of men came to Washington in response. They quickly filled up hotels and boarding houses, and eventually came to the White House. Soldiers from Kansas slept in

Abraham Lincoln endured a great deal of grief during his time in office.

the East Room, and more troops spilled out into the hallways. In 1863, history was made in the president's cabinet room – then on the second floor of the White House – when Lincoln signed the Emancipation Proclamation, which declared about four million slaves to be free.

FIRESIDE CHATS

Theodore Roosevelt's fifth cousin, Franklin D. Roosevelt, was president for 12 years and lived in the White House longer than any other president. From the White House, Roosevelt conducted regular 'fireside chats' that were broadcast on the radio. The chats were popular with the

President Franklin D. Roosevelt delivered regular broadcasts to the American people.

Tales & customs – WHO PAYS?

The general impression projected to the public is that the president and his family live like royalty in the White House. However, this is not strictly true. When food is purchased for an official White House function, the US government pays. But when the president, first lady, or their children want a personal meal or snack, they are charged for it. Few Americans realise that part of the president's salary goes towards the cost of food.

American children often become as familiar with White House pets as with their owners. The spaniel Rex is shown here with his owners, President Ronald and First Lady Nancy Reagan.

American public, giving them the feeling that he was accessible and that he wanted to come into their living rooms to talk with them. Roosevelt's wife, Eleanor, surprised the press and the public by holding press conferences for women reporters, who were not allowed to attend presidential press conferences. The conferences were usually held in the Red Room, and sometimes Mrs. Roosevelt would knit as she talked. Eleanor Roosevelt was an important first lady who became involved in many social and humanitarian programmes.

MISCHIEF-MAKING

Often, by the time the president and first lady came to the White House, their children were grown up and living away from home. But some presidents had young children who lived with them in the White House. President Abraham Lincoln's sons Willie and Tad were only 10 and eight when their father became president. They had great fun in the White House. For example, they would ring the servants' bells in different parts of the house to confuse the servants about where to go next. After his brother Willie died, President Lincoln bought Tad two goats, Nanny and Nanko, that Tad liked to bring inside the house and chase up and down the hallways. The Lincolns had other pets as well, including a turkey that President Lincoln had planned to kill and eat for Thanksgiving dinner. However, when the time came, Tad pleaded with his father to spare the turkey's life. The president agreed, and the Lincoln White House had another pet.

The Lincoln presidency was not the only time there were goats at the White House. President Harrison's grandchildren kept a pet goat called His Whiskers.

The White House

They hooked His Whiskers up to a cart, and the goat pulled them around White House grounds.

THE ROOSEVELT CLAN

Perhaps the most memorable presidential family was that of Theodore Roosevelt. Along with his wife, Edith, he had six children. The Roosevelt children filled the White House with happy noise, sometimes even chaos. They took metal trays from the kitchen and used them to slide down staircases, and they roller-skated down corridors throughout the mansion. One rainy afternoon, Quentin Roosevelt had two friends over to play, and they thought it would be fun to throw spitballs at the portraits of presidents hanging in the White House. When President Roosevelt saw the spitballs all over the paintings, he ordered Quentin and his friends to clean off every last one, and then decided Quentin could have no friends over to play until the president decided his punishment had lasted long enough. Quentin created more commotion when he took his pony, Algonquin, up to the second floor in the White House lift to cheer up his sick brother, Archie. To add to the hilarity in the White House, the Roosevelt clan had many other pets, including a lizard, guinea pigs, a pig, a badger, a hyena, a macaw and a rooster.

President Carter's daughter Amy is shown here sitting in the tree house her father designed for her in the White House grounds.

ENTERTAINING THE KIDS

In 1977, Jimmy Carter, became president. His daughter Amy was nine years old at the time, and the youngest of the Carter children. For the most part, she was the only child in the White House, so she had to find ways to amuse herself. President Carter designed a tree house for Amy in 1977. It was built on a platform on stilts among the trees on the South Lawn. When the Carters left the White House in 1981, the tree house was taken apart and put in White House storage, where it is kept as an historic object. Another daughter of a recent president, Chelsea Clinton, had a cat named Socks, and her father, Bill Clinton, was rarely seen without his chocolate Labrador, Buddy, by his side.

Theodore Roosevelt's son Quentin is remembered for mischief-making at the White House. He once took his pony up via the second floor lift to visit his sick brother.

Tales & customs – SUPREME SERVICE

First Lady Nancy Reagan wrote in her book My Turn: 'Every evening while I took a bath, one of the maids would come by and remove my clothes for laundering or dry cleaning. The bed would always be turned down. Five minutes after Ronnie [President Ronald Reagan] came home and hung up his suit, it would disappear from the closet to be pressed, cleaned or brushed. No wonder Ron used to call the White House an eight-star hotel.'

WHITE WEDDINGS

The White House has been the site of many joyous occasions throughout its history. Perhaps the most notable of these are the 17 weddings that took place there. The first wedding in the White House was in 1812, when Dolley Madison's sister, Lucy Payne Washington – she was the widow of George Washington's nephew – married Supreme Court Justice Thomas Todd. Only one president was married in the White House. He was Grover Cleveland, who entered the White House as a bachelor and married Frances Folsom in 1886. Frances was 27 years younger than President Cleveland – and at 21 years old was the youngest first lady ever. The wedding took place in the flower-filled Blue Room, and famous bandleader John Philip Sousa – who was director of the US Marine Band for 12 years – led the band in the *Wedding March*. Later, the Cleveland's second daughter, Esther, was the first and only president's child to be born in the White House.

President Grover Cleveland and Frances Folsom married at the White House in 1886. Cleveland was the only president to marry there while in office.

Richard Nixon's daughter Tricia was one of a few presidents' children to marry at the White House during their father's presidency.

PRESIDENTIAL DAUGHTERS

The daughters of several presidents have been married in the White House. The first was James Monroe's daughter Maria, whose wedding ceremony took place in 1820. In 1874 the wedding of Nellie Grant, daughter of President Ulysses S. Grant, to Algernon Sartoris took place in the East Room, with a wedding breakfast following in the State Dining Room. One wedding ceremony that fascinated the press – and the entire nation – was that of Alice Roosevelt, daughter of President Theodore Roosevelt. Nicknamed 'Princess Alice' by the press, the president's daughter had already captured the attention of America with her free-spirited and fun-loving nature. Her 1906 wedding to Ohio Congressman Nicholas Longworth received attention from around the world. The ceremony took place in the East Room, and the reception was in the State Dining Room. Other president's daughters who have been married in the White House include Tricia Nixon, who in 1971 married Edward Cox in the first White House Ceremony to be held in the rose garden.

SADNESS AND SORROW

The White House has also been the scene of great sorrow. Perhaps the most touching episode occurred on February 20, 1862,

when President Lincoln's son Willie died of typhoid. His parents were naturally devastated by his death, but Mrs. Lincoln, in particular, never really recovered.

Tales & customs – DEATHS IN THE WHITE HOUSE

Only two presidents have died inside the White House. They are William Henry Harrison, who died of pneumonia in 1841, and Zachary Taylor, who died in 1850 after suffering a bout of gastroenteritis. Several first ladies have died in the White House, including Letitia Tyler in 1842, Caroline Scott Harrison in 1892, and Ellen Wilson in 1914.

A very sad day for America. The procession bearing President John F. Kennedy's casket departed from the White House on November 25, 1963 after his untimely death by an assassin's bullet.

visiting a school in Florida at the time, but Vice President Dick Cheney was at the White House. Underneath the White House are underground bunkers to be used during times of national emergency, and on that day Cheney was rushed to one of these bunkers to ensure that he would be safe in case the White House or other government buildings were attacked. The bunker is called the PEOC, short for the Presidential Emergency Operations Center, and is fully equipped with the latest communications technology. Later, it was discovered that the White House was a likely target for the plane that crashed in Pennsylvania on September 11.

Willie's body was displayed in the Green Room, as far away from his mother's room as possible, and his funeral service was held in the East Room. Three years later, Abraham Lincoln's body was displayed in the same East Room. The victim of an assassin's bullet, Lincoln died on April 14, 1865.

Almost one hundred years later, the body of another assassinated president lay in state in the East Room. John F. Kennedy had been visiting Dallas, Texas, on November 22, 1963, when he was shot and killed by Lee Harvey Oswald. Kennedy's body was flown to Washington, D.C., and his flag-draped casket was displayed in the East Room on the same catafalque that had held Lincoln's body in 1865.

A DAY OF PURE TERROR

George W. Bush was president on September 11, 2001, when terrorists attacked the World Trade Center towers in New York City and the Pentagon in Washington, DC. Bush was

The sight of the burning twin towers of the World Trade Center sent a wave of shock across the western world.

CHAPTER 5

Significant events

The White House has played host to hundreds of special guests. They include dignitaries, heads of state, presidents and royal figures from around the world. Whatever the reason for their visit, these distinguished visitors would always be granted a comfortable and memorable stay courtesy of White House staff. Countless concerts, recitals and performances have taken place at the White House, in the style favoured by the president at the time.

First Lady Nancy Reagan made a point of sampling all dishes before they were served to any distinguished White House guests.

PLANNING

A great deal of planning goes into each state and official visit to the White House. Months before the visit is to occur, White House staff begin working out the details. They do research to find out what kinds of food the visiting dignitary likes, what his or her favourite colours and flowers are, and what kind of music the visitor enjoys.

They must also make sure that nothing would offend the visitor for religious or other reasons. For example, in China the colour white symbolises death and mourning, so white flowers would be avoided when guests from China are visiting. In the days leading up to the event, a detailed schedule of everything that is to occur during the visit is written and studied to make sure that nothing is left to chance. The White House Social Office even keeps extra hair dryers, hosiery, shoes and dresses in case a guest has an emergency need.

The head chef comes up with many ideas for dishes to serve for the occasion, and staff members, the first lady, and sometimes even the president all sample the food and provide opinions. On the days before the State Visit, staff members study the White House to make sure everything is in order, checking to make sure the

President Ford waltzed with Queen Elizabeth II at a State Dinner celebrating the American Bicentennial in 1976.

White House visits are divided into three types. State Visits are reserved for heads of state, such as kings, queens, and presidents. Official Visits are for prime ministers or other heads of government. The third category is Working Visits, which includes meetings with the president and his cabinet or with other members of government. State Visits and Official Visits require arrival ceremonies and State Dinners.

walls are cleanly painted and there are no scuff marks to be seen on the floors.

NOTABLE VISITORS

Among the notable visitors have been King David Kalakaua of the Sandwich Islands – now the state of Hawaii – who in 1874 was the first monarch to attend a State Dinner. During World War II, many dignitaries visited President Franklin D. Roosevelt to discuss the war, including King George and Queen Elizabeth of Great Britain, British Prime Minister Winston Churchill, the King of Greece, the Queen of Holland, and Madame Chiang Kai-Shek of China. The first pope to visit the White House was John Paul II, who arrived in 1979 during Jimmy Carter's presidency. Recent historic events at the White House include the signing of a peace treaty by Egypt's President Anwar Sadat and Israel's Prime Minister Menachim Begin in 1979, also during the Carter Administration. In the East Room

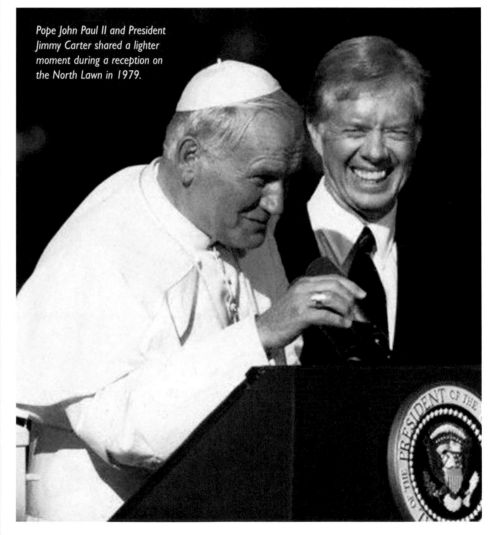

Pope John Paul II and President Jimmy Carter shared a lighter moment during a reception on the North Lawn in 1979.

in 1987, President Ronald Reagan and Soviet President Mikhail Gorbachev signed the world's first arms control agreement, called the Intermediate Nuclear Force Treaty, and in 1993,

President Clinton and 3,000 guests watched as Prime Minister Yitzhak Rabin of Israel and Palestine Liberation Organization Chairman, Yassar Arafat, signed a peace treaty on the South Lawn.

The White House

CULTURAL EVENTS

The White House has been the site of numerous concerts and other cultural events. The first reception at the White House was held in 1801, and the United States Marine Band played. Ever since, the band has made regular visits to the White House and is even called 'The President's Own'. During President Lincoln's administration, he arranged for the band to perform in the White House grounds every week.

The Kennedy Administration is remembered for the many important cultural events held in the White House during that time. Groups such as the Metropolitan Opera Studio, the American Shakespeare Festival, and Jerome Robbins Ballet performed at the White House, as did individual performers such as composer and conductor Leonard Bernstein and Pablo Casals. The Casals concert was considered ground-breaking because Casals had first played at the White House in 1904 but after 1938

Ballet performances are popular choices for family entertainment at the White House. The Washington Ballet Company performed a Christmas-themed ballet on this occasion, at the bidding of President George W. and First Lady Laura Bush. In the audience were children of military personnel stationed all over the world.

Tales & customs – ATHLETES AT THE WHITE HOUSE

Athletes and sports teams who have won their sports' highest honours are regularly invited to the White House. In 2003, for example, the winners of baseball's World Series, the Florida Marlins, were congratulated at the White House by President George W. Bush, as were the winners of the National Basketball Championship, the San Antonio Spurs. Individual athletes such as five-time Tour de France winner Lance Armstrong and Olympic medal winners have been honoured at the White House as well.

against communism in his country. The Clintons asked Lou Reed to perform and he agreed. He was accompanied by Czech bassist Milan Hlavsa. Musicians from other countries also perform at the White House. In 1916, President Woodrow Wilson enjoyed a concert by Australian pianist and composer Percy Grainger. For a visit by British Prime Minister Tony Blair, the Clintons asked Elton John to sing with American musician Stevie Wonder. Other performers have included Eric Clapton, cellist Yo-Yo Ma and U2 lead singer Bono, among many others.

One event that is held at the end of each year is a reception for recipients of the Kennedy Center Honors. These awards are for Americans who have made significant contributions to the performing arts. Among recent recipients are Bill Cosby, Shirley Temple Black, Jack Nicholson, and Loretta Lynn.

In 1798, the US Marine Band, shown here in 1996, was set up by President John Adams. The tradition has been maintained ever since and there are currently 143 musicians in the band.

refused to visit the United States because he disagreed with its policies toward his native country, Spain. He agreed to return and perform because he admired President John F. Kennedy. The concert was televised in the United States. Sometimes a guest will mention a favourite performer or even request someone specific. Among the many guests welcomed to the White House by President Bill Clinton and First Lady Hillary Clinton was President Vaclav Havel of the Czech Republic.

MANY MUSIC STYLES

When the president and first lady consider whom to ask to entertain at a State Dinner, they sometimes have difficulty deciding who would be best, but in the case of President Havel, it was easy. He had already told the Clintons about his admiration for American musician Lou Reed, whose music, he said, inspired him as he fought

Sir Elton John and Stevie Wonder were invited to perform together at the White House in honour of an official visit from British Prime Minister Tony Blair in 1998.

The White House

INAUGURATIONS

The ceremony during which the President of the United States takes the oath of office is called the inauguration. Only four presidents have taken the oath in the White House, while others have taken place in other government buildings, such as the US Capitol Building, also in Washington. The first was Rutherford B. Hayes, who took the oath on Saturday, March 3, 1877. Because the usual day for a president's inauguration at the time, March 4, was a Sunday, the ceremony was privately held in the Red Room of the White House. His public inauguration took place on Monday, March 5. President Franklin D. Roosevelt's fourth and final inauguration took

Franklin D. Roosevelt delivered his inaugural address to a crowd of thousands from the South Portico of the White House on January 20, 1945.

Tales & customs – 'THE PEOPLE WOULD RULE'

The following was written about Andrew Jackson's inauguration at the White House: 'Cut glass and china to the amount of several thousand dollars had been broken in the struggle to get the refreshments … Ladies fainted, men were seen with bloody noses … It is mortifying to see men with boots heavy with mud, standing on the damask-satin-covered chairs and sofas … But it was the People's day, and the People's President and the People would rule.'

place on the South Portico of the White House on January 20, 1945, possibly because Roosevelt used a wheelchair at the time, something he typically kept a secret from the American public. Roosevelt died that April, and his vice president, Harry S. Truman, took the oath of office in the Cabinet Room of the West Wing almost immediately.

The 1957 inauguration of Dwight D. Eisenhower took place privately in the White House in 1957 in the East Room. When Richard Nixon was forced to resign in August 1974, vice president Gerald Ford became president and took the oath of office in the East Room. When Ronald Reagan was sworn in on January 20, 1985, because it was a Sunday, he was sworn in privately in the North Entrance Hall and then publicly the next day.

THE JACKSON INAUGURAL RECEPTION

James and Dolley Madison began the tradition of holding inaugural

President Dwight Eisenhower and his wife, Mamie, responded to a cheering crowd during his inauguration in 1953.

receptions and balls at the White house, but after Lincoln's presidency, crowds became too large for the White House to accommodate. Perhaps the most memorable example of this was the Inaugural Reception of Andrew Jackson in 1829. Jackson wanted to be thought of as a man for the people, so he invited the public to the White House for refreshments and drinks after his inauguration. White House staff were shocked when huge mobs of people rushed into the White House, ate all the food, and broke dishes and glasses. Women fainted, men with muddy boots stood on White House furniture to get a better look at the president, and fights broke out as people argued over who would get the last drink or slice of cake. Finally, members of Jackson's staff formed a chain to keep the crowds away from the president, and he escaped out of a back door.

CHAPTER 6

A day in the life

The activities of each day at the White House depend on what the President and First Lady have scheduled and what is going on in the world. Some White House events, however, are fairly predictable. Staff members show up to do their jobs, some arriving as early as 7 am. There is always food to prepare, floors to be cleaned, and phones and mail to be answered. The White House buzzes with activity nearly every hour of the day.

The National Park Services are responsible for keeping the White House grounds immaculate. This includes trimming the White House tree each year.

BEHIND THE SCENES

It takes a lot of work to keep the White House – with its 132 rooms – clean and in good repair, especially with up to 6,000 tourists and other visitors arriving every day. The person in charge of the 90 full-time staff is called the Chief Usher.

The White House kitchen employs five chefs, plus kitchen staff. The Executive Chef is carefully selected by the First Lady. The cooking staff, along with all of the White House residence staff, remain when a new president moves into the White House. To prepare for a State Dinner, one of the chefs might visit the library to learn more about the country's foods and customs. The staff also make sure they are aware of any dietary restrictions guests may have.

Other behind-the-scenes staff include the Chief Floral Designer who is responsible for ensuring flower arrangements are fresh and watered. Along with other staff florists, he or she creates stunning centrepieces for events held at the White House. Because invitations to White House functions are traditionally handwritten, three calligraphers are on staff to produce the thousands of invitations that are posted each month. They also handwrite menus and place cards. The exterior walls of the White House and its grounds are part of the National Park Service The 7.2 hectares that make up the White House complex are carefully tended by gardeners employed by the National Park Service whose employees are also responsible for putting up the White House Christmas tree and decorating the grounds for the holidays.

The White House is open to the public except on Sunday and Monday, so tours are regularly conducted. Tourists have a choice of taking a self-guided tour where

The president's working day often involves long-haul international flights just for a meeting.

they can tour the mansion at their own pace, or they can take a guided tour by one of their congressman or senators if they give the representative's office at least eight weeks notice.

PRESS BRIEFINGS

Some other events that occur on a regular basis are press briefings. These are given every day and usually last no more than an hour. Generally, the president's press secretary conducts press briefings. His or her job is to act as a mouthpiece for the president and answer each question the way the president would, so it is vital for that person to stay on top of all the issues and maintain regular contact with the president and

his staff. The journalists who regularly attend these press briefings are called the White House Press Corps. Some of them have been performing this function for decades.

THE PRESIDENT'S WORK DAY

The president spends his days meeting advisers and attending meetings and functions. He may spend an entire day with members of his Cabinet, or he may fly to any one of the 50 states on business. Sometimes, the president goes abroad to meet with leaders of other nations. To make sure he can fit everything into a day, the president usually rises early and goes to bed early.

Scott McClellan, Press Secretary to President George W. Bush, answers reporters' questions at a press conference.

Tales & customs – THE FIRST LADY

The First Lady's responsibilities are many and varied. She helps staff members prepare for White House social functions and acts as hostesses at each one. Some First Ladies, such as Eleanor Roosevelt, have been deeply involved in social programmes and projects. The role of the First Lady is not clearly defined, and each woman brings her personality and attitude to the role. Most Americans, however, seem to believe that the First Lady's primary responsibility is to support her husband.

CHAPTER 7

Uncovering the past

The president's home is living history – where everything possible has been done to preserve the house itself, and the treasures and furnishings that have found their way there throughout the many presidencies. However, there have been so many renovations, improvements and additions to the White House – both structural and decorative – that, without the efforts of historians, archaeologists and engineers, it would be easy to forget the precious details of its various incarnations.

RELIC KITS

The only real excavation of the White House was ordered by Harry Truman in 1948. A committee of engineers determined that the mansion was deteriorating. On December 13, 1949, work crews began dismantling the inside of the White House. As they took apart the wooden floors, each floorboard was numbered so it could be replaced exactly where it was.

Many of the scraps from the broken pieces or from materials that were determined to be unnecessary to save were put into 'relic kits' and sold to the public. For example, one kit contained a chunk of pine. Another had a chunk of sandstone and a nail from the White House. The largest kit provided enough stone or brick to build a fireplace. Money from the kits helped to pay for the renovation.

During Harry Truman's presidency, the White House underwent its most comprehensive renovation ever. This involved pulling up floorboards and re-stabilising the foundations of the building.

Tales & customs – LINCOLN'S GHOST

Many people have reported seeing the ghost of Abraham Lincoln at the White House. British Prime Minister Winston Churchill even refused to sleep in the Lincoln Bedroom after claiming to have seen Lincoln's ghost in there. One of President Harrison's bodyguards claimed Lincoln's ghost kept him awake. He even went to a séance where he asked President Lincoln to stop walking around the White House.

HIDDEN BENEATH

As workers removed the interior walls of the White House, they revealed the interior lining that had been used to build the mansion in the 1790s and in the rebuilding after the 1814 fire. They saw that behind the exterior sandstone walls were several layers of brick that were sealed with whitewash. Work crews found a marble box that had been hidden under the Entrance Hall, and inside the box was a bottle of rye whisky. Historians believe the liquor was placed there during Prohibition years – 1919 to 1933 – when Americans were forbidden to buy alcohol. Workers also found a brick that had the imprint of a dog's paw – apparently a dog had stepped onto the damp brick during the original construction. Others found charred timbers and sandstone, evidence of the fire set by the British during the War of 1812. Labourers also saw that the inside of the exterior walls had

The White House requires regular waterblasting to remove dirt from the exterior. In the 1980s a thorough cleaning revealed many fine details.

ducts used by an old furnace heating system, as well as hand-powered bell systems that at one time were used to summon servants and staff. President Truman, who always enjoyed studying history, followed the demolition closely and was fascinated by the evidence of the White House in former years. He was particularly interested in seeing the marks left by the Scottish stonemasons, who had used their chisels to carve Masonic symbols into bricks and stone.

MYSTERY OF THE CORNERSTONE

In an attempt to find the cornerstone laid by the masons in a 1792 ceremony, Truman and architect Lorenzo Winslow searched the walls with a metal detector, which they hoped would locate a brass plaque said to be on the stone. They reported that the loudest buzz from the detector was at the southwest corner, but Truman was against destroying the exterior wall to reach it, so the exact location of the cornerstone is still a mystery.

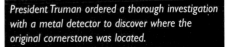

President Truman ordered a thorough investigation with a metal detector to discover where the original cornerstone was located.

CHAPTER 8

Preserving the past

Restoration is a constant requirement at the White House. Since Truman ordered the most comprehensive ever White House renovation project in the 1950s, many further alterations have taken place. During the 1990s, a Committee for Preservation of the White House was revived – with the purpose of determining what renovations were required and when. From this period onwards, restorative acts have included – among other things – the re-upholstering of 73 pieces of furniture and pillows, the repair of two floors and hanging new curtains or drapes in 28 windows.

A team of full-time architects and renovators ensure that the White House is constantly in prime condition.

TIME AND NATURE

The restoration was not funded by public funds but by private donations, much of them from the White House Historical Association. This association was formed in 1961 at the request of the National Park Service and with the encouragement of First Lady Jackie Kennedy. The association raises money by publishing and selling educational materials. In July 1962, among its first publications was *The White House: An Historic Guide*. An updated version of the book continues to be published today, and money from its sales goes to preserving the White House. The Clinton restoration was also funded by donations from the National Park Service, which maintains the White House and its grounds. Such donations are necessary, since presently the government gives each administration only $50,000 per administration to decorate the mansion.

Beginning in 1988, to coincide with the 200th anniversary of the laying of the White House cornerstone in 1992, architects and historians began a close examination of every part of the White House. They took notes and kept records of the sandstone blocks on the exterior of the building, then moved inside

Restoration at the White House in 1952 was finished a month ahead of schedule, and cost $5 million in total. The Presidential family moved back in to the building soon afterwards.

The restoration of pieces of furniture, such as this chair first purchased by President Monroe, ensure early pieces from the White House can remain in use.

The White House has been standing for more than 200 years and is perhaps the best-loved building in the United States. Fortunately, those who have worked so hard to become residents of the White House usually understand the responsibility, and respect its traditions and history. The White House symbolises fundamental values that the United States defines itself by: hard work, diversity and strength.

and studied each wall, door, window frame and piece of trim. They ended up with more than 850 pages that will be valuable in future renovation and restoration of the White House.

Tales & customs – A SENSE OF CONTINUITY

In 1901 Theodore Roosevelt said: *The White House is the property of the nation, and so far as it is compatible with living therein should be kept as it originally was, for the same reasons that we keep Mount Vernon [George Washington's home] as it originally was. . . . It is a good thing to preserve such buildings as historic monuments, which keep alive our sense of continuity with the nation's past.*

Glossary

Administration The government currently in power.

Advocate A person who publicly supports a cause or idea.

al-Qaeda An anti-western terrorist network that dispenses money, logistical support and training to a wide variety of radical Islamic terrorist groups. It has divisions in more than 50 countries.

Anglo-Palladian An 18th century architectural style combining the technique of 16th century Italian architect Andrea Palladio with English architectural styles.

Assassination The murder of a political, religious or celebrity figure.

Axis Powers The three countries, Germany, Italy, and Japan, which fought against the Allied Powers in World War II.

Barracks Large building or group of buildings for housing soldiers.

Bunker Heavily fortified underground chamber.

Cabinet Group of senior government ministers who act as an advisor to the president or prime minister.

Catafalque Ornamental platform on which a coffin is placed during a funeral.

Colonnade Regularly spaced columns supporting a roof.

Commissioner Representative with governmental authority.

Communism Political system where all property is owned by the community and each person contributes according to their ability and needs.

Confederacy The southern states of America that separated from the northern states in 1860–1. The northern states were known as the Union.

Congress A national law-making body.

Controversy Public debate about a matter which arouses strong public opinion.

Cornerstone Stone that forms the base of the corner of a building.

Curator Person who is responsible for caring for a place where item are exhibited, such as a museum.

Declaration of Independence A document signed on July 4, 1776 that declared the United States of America to be independent of the British Crown.

Decommission Remove or withdraw from active service.

Décor A decorative style or scheme, such as would be applied to a room.

Democracy Form of government where the people have a say in who runs the country and which policies are introduced as law.

Dignitary Person who holds a high position or rank.

Diplomat Someone who is responsible for conducting negotiations between nations.

Dumb waiter A small elevator used to transport food or other small items from one floor to another using a pulley system.

Emancipation Freedom from legal, social or political restrictions.

Emancipation Proclamation The law passed in 1862 that officially ended slavery in the United States of America.

Empire Style Neoclassical style of clothing, architecture and the decorative arts that developed in France in the early 19th century during Napoleon Bonaparte's rule.

It was meant to visually reflect the harmony of all things under Napoleon's leadership.

Façade Front or exterior of a building.

Gastro-enteritis Illness in which the person suffers inflammation of the lining of the stomach and intestines.

Great Depression The worldwide economic crisis beginning with the stock market crash in 1929 and continuing throughout the 1930s.

Hors d'oeuvres Food served as appetisers.

Humanitarian Concerned with human rights and welfare.

Inauguration Ceremony held to swear someone into governmental office.

Judicial Branch of government that interprets the law and includes the court system.

Legislative Branch of government that makes laws.

Marquee Large tent used for outdoor parties.

Mortifying Causing to experience shame, humiliation or wounded pride.

NATO (North Atlantic Treaty Organization) An organisation created in 1949 for the purpose of international security.

Negotiations Discussions aimed at reaching an agreement.

Opalescent Something that reflects iridescent light.

Pentagon Headquarters of US military leadership.

Portico Entryway with a series of columns.

Reforms Make changes to something to improve it.

Revolutionary War Took place from 1775 to 1783 when the American colonies fought for independence from British rule.

Secretary of State In the US government, person who is responsible for foreign affairs.

Senate The upper house of the US Congress, to which two members are elected from each state by popular vote for a six year term.

Sovereign Person with supreme power in a government.

Successor A person or thing that succeeds another.

Symmetrical Balanced; when looked at straight on, having the same lines and angles on both sides.

Terrorist Person who uses violence, assassinations and intimidation to achieve political aims.

United Nations International organisation set up in 1945 consisting of over 150 countries to promote international peace, security and cooperation.

Watergate A series of scandals during the Nixon administration in which members of the executive branch committed illegal espionage against their opponents and were charged with violation of the public trust, bribery, contempt of Congress, and attempted obstruction of justice.

Weapons of mass destruction Nuclear and radiological weapons and explosive devices, and chemical and biological weapons.

Index

Copyright © ticktock Entertainment Ltd 2005
First published in Great Britain in 2005 by ticktock Media Ltd.,
Unit 2, Orchard Business Centre, North Farm Road, Tunbridge Wells, Kent, TN2 3XF
We would like to thank: Alison Howard, Susan Barraclough, Elizabeth Wiggans and Jenni Rainford for their help with this book.
Printed in China. A CIP catalogue record for this book is available from the British Library.

Picture Credits
AA World Travel Library: Alamy: 4–5; Associated Press Ltd: 13, 14L, 16L, 16R, 20BL, 21R, 22TL, 36–37, Art Archive: 4B, 10, 26, 28L, 38L, Bridgeman Art Library: 4T, 6L, 8–9, 11L, Corbis: 5R, 11R, 12T, 12B, 14R, 15, 17, 20R, 21BL, 22BL, 23TR, 23B, 24TR, 24BL, 24BR, 25R, 27BR, 29L, 29R, 30B, 30T, 31, 32L, 32–33, 34L, 34–35, 35R, 36L, 37B, 38R, 39, 40, 41BL, 41TR, 44–45; Getty Images: 18–19; Library of Congress: 6–7, 7R, 18L, 19T, 27TL; Robin Kent: 9R, Truman Library: 42